# LEADING TO BUILD GREAT TEAMS

# AIM FOR THE
# HEART

## TOM MATHEWS

### FOREWORD BY MAC ANDERSON

Cover Photo: Ken Jenkins
Design: Rich Nickel
Editor: Jennifer Svoboda

Printed and bound in the United States of America.

www.simpletruths.com

04  WOZ O8

# TABLE OF CONTENTS

Vince Lombardi, in his last speech before he died, was addressing a large corporate audience. He said, "I'm going to share with you the key to success in any business." You could have heard a pin drop as they sat on the edges of their seats waiting for the answer. He said, "The secret, in a word is…heartpower. ***Capture the heart, you've captured the person*** …Get people to fall in love with your company."

This is a very simple, powerful concept. But how does a leader do it? In my opinion, it starts and ends with caring about your people, not as employees, but as human beings.

Tom Mathews epitomizes a leader who understands what people want. He has built an amazing team of over **20,000** people through hard work and showing that he cares.

I first met Tom when he invited me to speak to his team at World Financial Group in Atlanta. Right away, I could tell that he is a leader who "gets it." He truly understands the power of recognition, kindness, and personal goals. Also, in all of his conversations, it was never "me" but always "we" when discussing any success he had enjoyed. In observing, I could feel the admiration and respect his people had for him. Time after time, I heard them say…"Thank you, Tom…your friendship, and your leadership has made a difference in my life."

I once heard a leader defined as "someone who knows the way, goes the way and shows the way"…Tom qualifies in all three! *Aim For The Heart* offers powerful lessons about leadership and what it takes to build great teams.

Read it. Enjoy it. And, most importantly LIVE IT.

All the best,
**Mac Anderson**
*Founder, Simple Truths and Successories*

# "YOU MUST CAPTURE AND KEEP THE HEART OF THE ORIGINAL AND SUPREMELY ABLE MAN BEFORE HIS BRAIN CAN DO ITS BEST."

These words were spoken by the great industrialist, Andrew Carnegie, and … I couldn't agree more. When I think back on the people who have motivated and inspired me in my business career, there were people who cared about me as a human being first and foremost. They cared about my family, my goals, my dreams; and, as my leader, helped show me how I could make my dreams come true. They "aimed for my heart," and I never forgot. I promised myself that if I ever had the opportunity to lead others, the heart would always come first, and that good things would follow.

When Andrew Carnegie was asked what he would do if he had to start over, he quickly replied, "Take away all my factories and money… just leave me with my good men and I'll get back in no time." I, like Carnegie, know that I can always replace material possessions but my most precious assets are the members of our great team. The passion of Bill Mitchell, the relationship savvy of Greg Sorensen, the people skills of Marcy Blochowiak, and the contributions of every senior leader on our team make our business family all it can be.

The leadership principals that I share in this book are the result of observing great leaders in action; and, of course, what I've learned in hiring, training and inspiring our team during the past 20 years. If you're an entrepreneur, or a manager, it is my hope that this book will become a place you can go when you've had a tough day and need a shot of inspiration. I also hope it can become a practical tool to help you:

> *Build relationships of trust*
> *Lead from the front*
> *Manage your attitude*
> *Know the power of stories*
> *Show sincere appreciation*
> *Make your team's goals exciting*
> *Sell your vision!*

When I was just getting started in business, I was worried about making it. Now, I worry more about making a difference. I sincerely hope that this book, in some small way, will make a difference in your life as a leader and a person.

Hope all your dreams come true!
**Tom Mathews**

# BUILD RELATIONSHIPS OF TRUST

# LIFE MOVES PRETTY FAST, BUT IN THE END IT'S ALL ABOUT OUR FAITH, OUR FAMILY, AND THE RELATIONSHIPS WE'VE FORMED ALONG THE WAY.

*Leading with the heart* is about many things. It's about caring, it's about setting team goals, it's about walking the talk, but there is nothing more relevant and satisfying than building relationships of trust. Life moves pretty fast, but in the end it's all about our faith, our family, and the relationships we've formed along the way. In comparison, nothing else comes close to these three things.

I graduated from St. Xavier High School and Xavier University in Cincinnati, Ohio with a major in accounting and a minor in life. A Jesuit education taught me so much during my eight years with them, but what I remember most is the relationships I formed along the way. Last year, during the holidays, I received the XU alumni magazine.

Father Michael Graham, S.J., President of Xavier, was talking about the University's annual Athletic Hall of Fame Induction. The Musketeer's recent men's basketball success has given them national attention – they made the Elite Eight last year in the NCAA Tournament and came within a few points of the Final Four. He wrote about the recent inductees speaking at the ceremony. He said, "What was surprising to us in attendance, however, was how little each of the inductees spoke about sports. Instead they talked about what they remembered most – about classmates and, especially, teammates. They talked about the example their parents set for them and how they couldn't possibly have achieved what they achieved – let alone be where they are today – absent the interest that so many others took in them. They reminded us all – and reminded us vividly – that not one of us ever accomplishes anything on our own. For all of us are webbed more deeply into a world of relationships than we could ever imagine. And that's a good thing to be reminded of because it poses an important question… *who is there around me right now who I might influence for the better?*"

Ken Blanchard, in his book, *The Servant Leader*, says, "We all need 'truth-tellers' in our lives. Trusted relationships provide our greatest opportunity to stay positive, stay focused and to grow."

# DEVELOP A HUNGER FOR LEARNING

IN ORDER TO LEAD EFFECTIVELY,
A PERSON MUST FIRST KNOW HOW TO LIVE
TO MAKE A DIFFERENCE IN THEIR OWN LIFE,
LEARN HOW TO MAKE A DIFFERENCE
IN OTHER PEOPLE'S LIVES,
AND, MOST IMPORTANTLY, LEAD TO MAKE A DIFFERENCE
THROUGH ETHICS AND INTEGRITY.
– DON SODERQUIST

*Of all the great business people* I've ever read about, Sam Walton was the most inquisitive and eager to learn. In fact, there was nothing he enjoyed more than going into a competitor's store trying to learn something from it. He wanted to be the best, and he knew that without continuous upgrades in merchandising, systems and products his competition would pass him by.

Don Soderquist, now Chairman of Wal-Mart, first met Sam in 1964. Don worked for Ben Franklin, and Sam, who had opened his first Wal-Mart, was in Chicago trying to convince Ben Franklin to franchise his discount stores in small towns. They thought he was crazy and gave him a flat "no." After the meeting, Don said Sam began asking him about computers... and was writing everything on his yellow legal pad.

17

The next Saturday, Don was shopping at K-Mart and looked up and saw Sam grilling the clerk…"Well, how frequently do you order?…Uh-huh…How much do you order? …And, if you order on Tuesday when does it come in?" Then he saw Sam on his hands and knees measuring the aisles and crawling under one of the stock tables. Finally Soderquist asked, "Sam is that you?" And Sam looked up from the floor and said, "Oh, Don, what are you doing here?" Don said, "I'm shopping. What are you doing?" "Oh," Sam said, "just part of the education process."

One of Walton's greatest sources of learning was his Saturday morning meetings at the Bentonville, Arkansas headquarters. Each Saturday at 7:30 a.m. members of his team met to discuss and debate much of their philosophy and management strategy. It became the focal point of all their communication efforts …and the very heart of the Wal-Mart culture.

The purpose of these meetings was to have some fun, but also to let everyone know what the rest of the company was up to. These meetings were also an opportunity to find heroes among their associates and bring them to Bentonville to sing their praises. They also discussed problems and opportunities to improve. However, Sam knew that he couldn't expect people to want to come week in and week out, so he always invited entertainment and encouraged the unpredictable. One week, he might invite comedian Jonathan Winters, and the next it might be singer Garth Brooks or somebody like Jack Welch, the CEO of General Electric. And for that reason they never had an agenda. Sam might just call on someone and say. "Okay, George, you conduct the meeting today." Of course, Sam always had a few things on his yellow pad that he'd toss out for discussion, and he always took notes at a furious pace as people discussed their perceived problems and opportunities. The Saturday meetings were often the place where Wal-Mart might first decide to try things that were considered unattainable. And instead of everybody shooting it down right away, they would figure out a way to make it work.

Sam Walton was an American original who founded, what is today, the largest company in the world. *There is no doubt that his competitive spirit and passion to learn was one of the keys to his success.*

**D**FOR YOUR WILDEST **D**REAMS TO COME TRUE YOU MUST HAVE WILD DREAMS

*I have always been a dreamer.* My imagination has been strong since I was a child. Early in my career, I was struggling to make a living. However, this didn't hinder my dreams for success. In fact, many Sundays I would go to the Mercedes-Benz dealership when they were closed and just walk around the lot imagining what it would feel like to drive a car like that. I was naïve enough to think anything was possible if I could dream it.

Shortly after this, I began attaching positive affirmations to my mirror. First I cut out the picture of the car of my dreams, and then I attached a piece of paper with three of my goals: 1) to become a $100,000 per year earner, 2) to become the #1 leader in my state, and 3) to become a senior executive in the company. The power of dreams and visualization worked for me, and within six months I was fortunate enough to achieve all three goals. Today, I'm 45 and can still say with passion that anything is possible if you can dream it.

Since the beginning of history, all of the world's most important achievements have started with a dream. In most instances the naysayers will line up to tell you it can't be done. *But dreams fuel passion, and passion plus perseverance can equal success.*

Shortly after Orville Wright flew his historic first flight at Kitty Hawk, a North Carolina reporter asked if everything was like he thought it would be. He said, "Actually, I preferred the dreaming of flying to doing it. I would lie in my bed at night and imagine the wind passing by, the view from above like a bird, and the exhilaration of it all."

As a leader, you must know and teach the power of dreams. Every member of your team must truly understand, as Carl Sandburg said,

## "NOTHING HAPPENS
## BUT FIRST A DREAM."

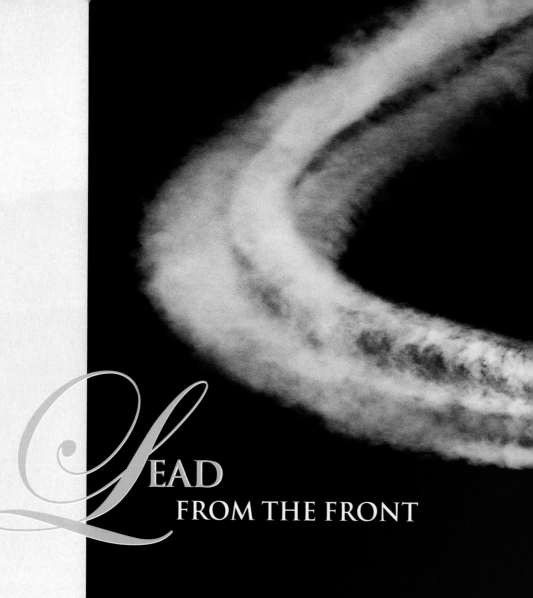

# LEAD
## FROM THE FRONT

*Andrew Carnegie* once said, "As I grow older I pay less attention to what people say. I just watch what they do." Leadership is not a birthright. It must be earned. One of the most important ways you earn it is to lead by example. The great Dr. Albert Sweitzer was once asked if he thought that setting an example was the most important quality of leadership. He paused and said, *"No, it's not the most important quality... it's the only one."*

Recently, I read a great story in *INC.* magazine written by Norm Browsky. In it, Browsky wrote about being on a Jet Blue flight when their CEO David Neeleman was on board.

"As we were buckling up to take off, Neeleman stood up and introduced himself. 'Hi, I'm Dave Neeleman, the CEO of Jet Blue. I'm here to serve this evening and I'm looking forward to meeting every one of you before we land.'

"As he was handing out snack baskets he would stop to chat with everyone. When he came to me, I told him I thought it was a great idea to serve his customer first hand, and asked him how often he did it. Expecting him to say once or twice a year, he said, 'Not often enough...I get to do it about once a month.'

"'Doing it,' he said, 'has been invaluable and many of our best ideas have come from talking with our customers.' He said, 'They're not shy, they tell me what they want.' By the end of the flight he had spoken to every passenger on the plane. Out of curiosity, I watched him interact with other passengers. In several instances, I saw him taking notes and listening intently to what passengers were saying. In a few instances when he couldn't answer the question, I watched him take a business card and say, 'Someone will be in touch with you in the next 24 hours.' Even at the end of the flight when the flight attendants asked the passengers to help by checking their seat pockets for trash, Neeleman, with his blue apron, was leading the charge."

This is a terrific story about how one leader has chosen to lead from the front. There is no doubt in my mind that every Jet Blue employee knows he "walks the talk." They also know that Dave Neeleman understands first hand what's happening on the front lines. *He's on their team.*

KNOW THAT
TEAMWORK
MAKES THE
DREAM WORK

*One person does not an organization make.* The power of any organization starts and ends with people. In fact, talented people committed to a common cause are unstoppable. Successories has a beautiful photograph of rowers at dusk with the following message underneath:

TEAMWORK IS THE ABILITY
TO WORK TOGETHER
TOWARD A COMMON VISION.

THE ABILITY TO DIRECT INDIVIDUAL
ACCOMPLISHMENT TOWARD
ORGANIZATIONAL OBJECTIVES.

IT IS THE FUEL THAT ALLOWS
COMMON PEOPLE TO OBTAIN
UNCOMMON RESULTS.

For any leader to succeed they must truly understand the power of teamwork and its potential for rewards.

In 1996, runner Michael Johnson, at the Atlanta Olympics, set an Olympic record in the 400-meter and beat his own world record in the 200-meter. He became the first man ever to win both events in the same Olympic Games. Our company was a corporate sponsor and I was in the crowd at the finish line for that race. The Atlanta Olympic Games also held a 4x100-meter relay. Four individuals cover a single lap around the track, each contributing a quarter of the distance required. Relay races are a combination of speed and coordination.

The comparison of individual versus team accomplishments has never been more obvious than here. While Michael Johnson, the winner of 55 consecutive 400-meter finals, is one of the best ever at this distance, he proved NO MATCH for the collective efforts of four team members. Even though he dominated the individual distance, his times fade when compared to the time required for four less qualified individuals to cover the same distance in a relay manner. Both the men's and women's teams outperformed the all-time individual champion.

Individual accomplishment is no match for a tightly unified, committed team. Teamwork is about sharing the load and accomplishing what individually is beyond reach. Here is the reality of teamwork:

MICHAEL JOHNSON'S 1996 400-METER OLYMPIC RECORD:
**43.49 seconds**

WOMEN'S 4x100-METER OLYMPIC RECORD:
**41.60 seconds**

MEN'S 4x100-METER OLYMPIC RECORD:
**37.40 seconds**

In 1970, I began playing the trumpet, and have enjoyed music ever since. I learned then that if everyone plays the same note you cannot have harmony or beautiful music. Over the years, in business, that lesson has come in handy many times. No matter what team you are a part of, each person has a unique note to play. This combination, just like a great band with many instruments, can make beautiful music.

KNOW
THE
POWER OF
STORIES

***Author and speaker Tom Peters*** recently said, "I stopped giving presentations years ago. Now I only tell stories." He says, "As I prepare I am conscious — 100% of time — of the evolving story, of the plot, of the narrative that unfolds. Whoever has the best story wins — so work on your story!"

Peter's advice should be taken to heart by any leader striving to build a great team. Stories are the ultimate communication tool. In fact, some of our greatest presidents ... Abe Lincoln, Teddy Roosevelt and Ronald Reagan were master storytellers ... used stories to ***inspire, encourage and educate us.*** As a leader, to capture the heart of your team, there is nothing more powerful than the right story at the right time.

An example of this is a story about a Native American boy who was talking to his grandfather:

*"What do you think about the world situation?"*
*the young boy asked.*

*The grandfather replied, "I feel like wolves are fighting in my heart. One is full of anger and hatred; the other is full of love, forgiveness, and peace."*

*"Which one will win?" asked the boy.*

*To which the grandfather replied, "The one I feed."*
*(Origin Unknown)*

The simple story makes the powerful point that, in life, *you become what you think about.* I could talk for an hour about this life-changing law and not capture the essence more clearly than by telling this 30-second story. Every organization has core values that its leaders should continually reinforce; not with words, but with stories.

TO LIVE

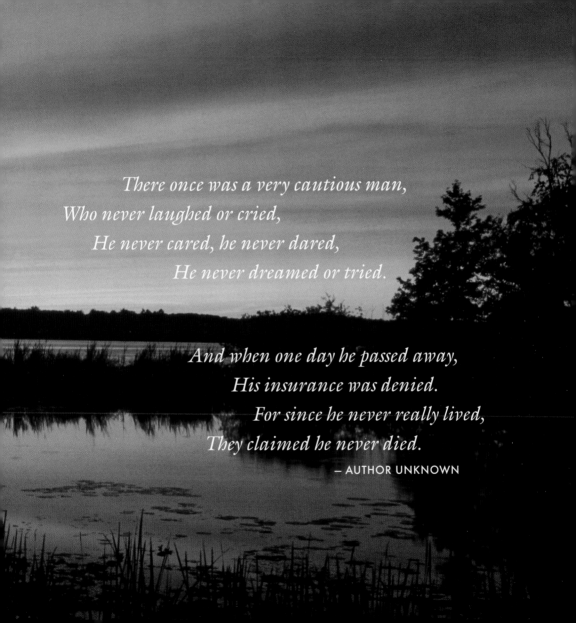

*There once was a very cautious man,*
*Who never laughed or cried,*
*He never cared, he never dared,*
*He never dreamed or tried.*

*And when one day he passed away,*
*His insurance was denied.*
*For since he never really lived,*
*They claimed he never died.*

— AUTHOR UNKNOWN

*"People are like sticks of dynamite.* The power is on the inside, but nothing happens until the fuse gets lit." What a great quote, and every leader should take it to heart. Deep inside we all want people in our lives who will help to make us all we can be. You can be that person for the members of your team. Providing timely encouragement, recognition and support will help to light the fuse... and, in many instances, unleash their emotional energy.

*I recently read a wonderful story* about a young man who played for the legendary Alabama football coach, Bear Bryant. Bear had a third stringer on his team named Henry Peterson. Henry had never gotten to play, and just before the Alabama-Auburn Game, Bryant got a call from Henry. He said, "Coach, my Dad died and I won't be able to make it to the game on Saturday." Bear said, "No problem, son, you should be with your family." However, the next day Bear got another call from Henry, and he said, "Coach, I got to thinking about it and I don't want to let the team down. I'm going to be there." Sure enough on Saturday, Henry was dressed and ready to play. Just before the game he walked over to Bear and said, "Coach, I want you to start me today." Bear said, "Son, are you nuts? This is the Alabama-Auburn game, and you've never played." Well, Henry persisted, and Bryant, never knowing why, said, "Okay, I'll put you in on the first play."

Henry Peterson scored three touchdowns in the first half ... he almost beat Auburn by himself. Bear, at halftime, walked over and said, "Son, I don't know whether to kiss you or kill you. Why haven't you shown me you can play football like that?" Henry said, "Coach, did you ever see me walking around the campus with my Dad?" Bear said, "Yes, I have seen you." Henry then said, "Coach, my Dad was blind and today is the first day he ever got to watch me play football."

## AS A LEADER, YOU CAN NEVER UNDERESTIMATE THE POWER OF EMOTIONAL ENERGY.

One timely shot of inspiration can quickly change negative thoughts into positive results for a member of your team. You must always ask yourself, "Am I doing all I can to help them become all they can be?"

*L*ESS CAN BE MORE

# JUST DO WHAT YOU DO BEST.
### – RED AUERBACH

*Two of the all-time greatest coaches* in sports history were Red Auerbach, who coached the great Boston Celtics basketball team in the 1950s and 1960s, and Vince Lombardi, the legendary football coach for the Green Bay Packers. When I read their biographies, what struck me most was their *"keep it simple"* philosophy. While other coaches were teaching complicated offense and defense, both Lombardi and Auerbach only had a few plays, but here was the key ... they executed the plays to perfection.

WINNING IS
NOT A SOMETIME THING;
IT'S AN ALL TIME THING.

YOU DON'T WIN ONCE IN A WHILE,
YOU DON'T DO THINGS
RIGHT ONCE IN A WHILE,
YOU DO THEM RIGHT ALL THE TIME.

WINNING IS A HABIT.
UNFORTUNATELY, SO IS LOSING.

— VINCE LOMBARDI

Someone once asked Auerbach what magic formula he had for winning games. He laughed and said, "Our secret to success is what I would call 'effective simplicity.' Nothing complicated. In fact, we only have seven different plays, and Bill Russell touched the ball on every one of them."

Under Auerbach's "effective simplicity" philosophy, the Boston Celtics won every championship from 1959 through 1966 – eight years in a row, a record unmatched since.

Lombardi's coaching philosophy was strikingly similar, and he had only five running plays in his offense, but like Auerbach, executed every play to perfection. He'd often say, "We really don't fool anyone. The opposition knows what's coming but they rarely stop us because every player knows his assignment because we've practiced it a thousand times." Lombardi was fanatical when it came to teaching and reinforcing the basic fundamentals of the game. In his mind, blocking and tackling were the keys to winning football games. In fact, to make his point on fundamentals, every year he would begin his training camp by saying … *"Gentlemen, this is a football."*

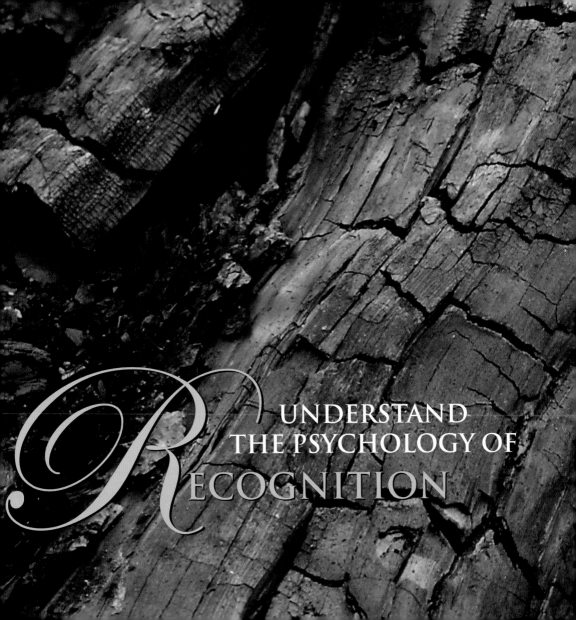

UNDERSTAND
THE PSYCHOLOGY OF
*R*ECOGNITION

***To understand why recognition is important*** we must understand its role in motivating people.

First of all, what is motivation? The definition I like is: "An inner drive that compels behavior." The subject has been studied for years, and as far back as Aristotle and Plato, many theories have come forth about why certain people are highly motivated to achieve and others simply don't care. In the simple definition above, the key word is "inner." Motivation is a complex subject because all motivation comes from within, and since we're all different...well, need I say more?

Noted psychologist Dr. Abraham Maslow provided the most popular theory on motivation and its impact on human behavior. He wrote that all human beings have a hierarchy of needs that control behavior. Once our physical needs are met (i.e. food, water, shelter) we are motivated by what he calls our basic human needs. In Maslow's hierarchy, recognition, or the desire to feel important in the eyes of others, plays a key role in influencing our behavior at home and in the workplace.

➤ THE NEED FOR SECURITY,
    *to feel safe.*

➤ THE NEED FOR RECOGNITION,
    *what I do is important to others.*

➤ THE NEED FOR ACCEPTANCE,
    *what I am is important to others.*

➤ THE NEED FOR NEW EXPERIENCES,
    *to grow.*

THE HUMAN SPIRIT IS
    NURTURED BY PRAISE,
AS MUCH AS A SEEDLING
    IS NURTURED BY THE SOIL,
      THE WATER AND THE SUN.
          —MARIO FERNANDEZ

# LISTEN
## FOR SUCCESS

*Steve Shapiro* is a speaker and author who recently made the decision to focus all of his time and resources on teaching organizations the "art" of listening. In Steve's opinion (and mine, as well), listening determines, more than any other factor, the quality of your communication and thus your success as a leader. Gallop recently polled over a million employees, and of those that thought they had a great boss, Gallop asked the question, "why?" *And the number one reason people thought their boss was great was that they were willing to listen* to what they had to say. Shapiro says, "When we listen, really listen to people deeply, something shifts. You can sense it. It transfers the relationship on the spot. If you think about the people you really enjoy being with, I'll guarantee you one thing... they are good listeners!

The next time someone comes to you with a problem to discuss, Shapiro offers this advice:

*"Focus your attention solely on the individual and allow no interruptions. Encourage them to relax and let them talk at their own pace. Leave them room to breathe as they sort through their emotions and their words."*

In the end, pause briefly with what he calls a Golden Silence. This sends the message that you, the listener, care enough to take it in and consider what they had to say.

Most leaders I know grossly underestimate the power of being a great listener. It is a quality that can be learned, but it takes patience and desire to get better. Breaking old habits is never easy. Desire is key, because the best definition of listening I've ever heard is … *"Listening is wanting to hear."* It is an emotional, not a physical process.

On a lighter note, Teddy Roosevelt, one of our great presidents, was known as an excellent listener. One of his pet peeves was people exchanging small talk and not listening to what was being said. He decided to conduct an experiment at a White House reception one evening. When the first three people walked though the line, Roosevelt looked them in the eye and said, "Good evening, I just killed my grandmother." They each said "Good evening, Mr. President, it's great to meet you, too!" However, when he said it to the fourth gentleman, the man stopped and looked a little stunned. He then bent over and whispered in Roosevelt's ear, "She probably deserved it." Roosevelt laughed and let him in on his little secret.

Develop the art of listening. It will deliver a tremendous return on whatever time you're willing to invest.

AS A LEADER, WHAT ARE YOU DOING
TO MANAGE YOUR MOST IMPORTANT ASSET...
YOUR ATTITUDE?

# MANAGING YOUR ATTITUDE

*There is nothing more important* to leading your team than maintaining a positive attitude. It's not easy, and it's a very personal thing ... but it must be done. We all have times when doubts, fears and negative thoughts creep into our thinking. When that happens, the key is to know yourself well enough to be able to change the way you feel. Emotional "triggers" can help us do that. For some, just hearing their favorite songs will do it. For others, it might happen by re-reading a personal letter or looking at a certain family photo.

For me, however, what works best is just to remind myself how blessed I am. I live in a great country. I have a wonderful family and wonderful friends I can turn to for support. I continually remind myself to worry less about what I don't have and to be thankful for what I do … to live with gratitude.

The following is something I keep in my desk and read from time to time to keep my attitude in focus. I'll share it with you:

*If the Earth's population were shrunk into a village of just 100 people – with all the human ratios existing in the world still remaining – what*

*would this tiny, diverse village look like? That's exactly what Phillip Harter, a medical doctor at the Stanford University School of Medicine, attempted to figure out. This is what he found…*

| | |
|---|---|
| 57 | WOULD BE ASIAN |
| 21 | WOULD BE EUROPEAN |
| 14 | WOULD BE FROM THE WESTERN HEMISPHERE |
| 8 | WOULD BE AFRICAN |
| 52 | WOULD BE FEMALE |
| 48 | WOULD BE MALE |
| 70 | WOULD BE NON-WHITE |
| 30 | WOULD BE WHITE |
| 70 | WOULD BE NON-CHRISTIAN |
| 30 | WOULD BE CHRISTIAN |
| 80 | WOULD LIVE IN SUBSTANDARD HOUSING |
| 70 | WOULD BE UNABLE TO READ |
| 50 | WOULD SUFFER FROM MALNUTRITION |
| 1 | WOULD HAVE A COLLEGE EDUCATION |

Think of it this way…if you live in a good home, have plenty to eat and can read, you are a member of a very select group. And if you have a good house, food, can read and have a computer, you are among the very elite. If you woke up this morning with more health than illness…you are more fortunate than the million who will not survive this week. If you have never experienced the danger of battle, the loneliness of imprisonment, the agony of torture, or the pangs of starvation…you are ahead of 500 million people in the world. If you can attend a church meeting without fear of harassment, arrest, torture, or death… you are fortunate, because more than three billion people in the world can't. If you have food in the refrigerator, clothes on your back, a roof over your head and a place to sleep…you are richer than 75% of the world. If you can read these words, you are more blessed than over two billion people in the world who cannot read at all.

*We are all very blessed* in some way, but occasionally we need to be reminded. For me, when I get a little down or when negative thoughts begin to creep in, I take out that little sheet of paper and read what is written above. *It quickly brings my life and my blessings into perspective.*

THE
POWER OF
PURPOSE

> # THE PURPOSE OF LIFE
> # IS A LIFE OF PURPOSE.
> ## —RALPH WALDO EMERSON

***When we think*** about the history of this great country we live in; when we think about many of our leaders such as George Washington, Abraham Lincoln, and Franklin Roosevelt, we see that they were all inspired by a powerful purpose. That purpose was Freedom.

I recently saw a copy of an article written by Ms. Cormel Nistorescu in a Romanian newspaper. It was titled *"C'ntorea Americili,"* meaning *"Ode to America,"* and was published September 24, 2001. I think you'll find it interesting.

*"Why are Americans so united?* They would not resemble one another even if you painted them all one color! They speak all the languages of the world and form an astonishing mixture of civilizations and religious beliefs. Still, the American tragedy (the events of September 11, 2001) turned three hundred million people into a hand put on the heart.

"Nobody rushed to accuse the White House, the army, and the secret services that they are only a bunch of losers. Nobody rushed to empty their bank accounts. Nobody rushed out onto the streets nearby to gape about. The Americans volunteered to donate blood and to give a helping hand.

"After the first moments of panic, they raised their flag over the smoking ruins, putting on T-shirts, caps and ties in the colors of the national flag. They placed flags on buildings and cars as if in every place and on every car a government official or the president was passing.

"On every occasion, they started singing their traditional song: 'God Bless America'! I watched the live broadcast and rerun after rerun for hours listening to the story of the guy who went one hundred floors with a woman in a wheelchair without knowing who she was, or of the Californian hockey player who gave his life fighting with the terrorists and prevented the plane from hitting a target that could have killed other hundreds or thousands of people.

"How on earth were they able to respond united as one human being? Imperceptibly, with every word and musical note, the memory of some turned into a modern myth of tragic heroes. And with every phone call, millions and millions of dollars were put in a collection aimed at rewarding not a man or a family, but a spirit, which no money can buy.

"What on earth can unite the Americans in such a way? Their land? Their galloping history? Their economic power? Money? I tried for hours to find an answer, humming songs and murmuring phrases with the risk of sounding commonplace.

"I thought things over, but I reached only one conclusion…

### FREEDOM CAN WORK SUCH MIRACLES."

# SELL YOUR VISION

**Author Warren Benis said,** "Leadership is the capacity to turn vision into reality." However, having the vision is not enough...it must be sold. Quite frankly, this is an area where many leaders fall short. The mission, the vision, may be crystal clear in their minds, but they forget that the team needs continuous reinforcement to keep it in focus.

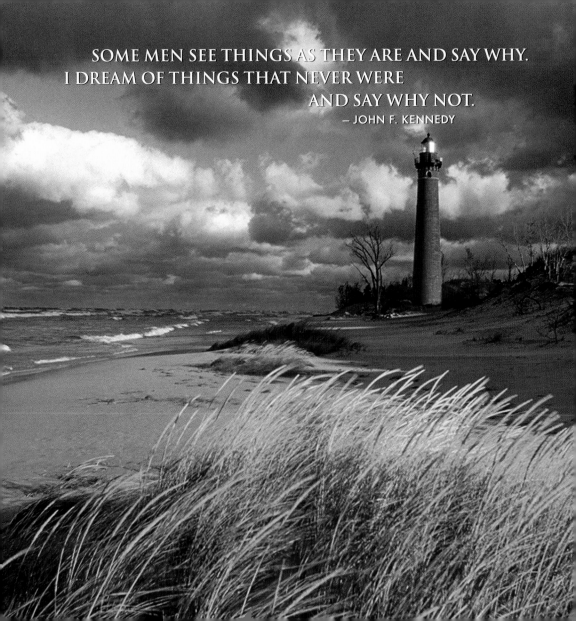

SOME MEN SEE THINGS AS THEY ARE AND SAY WHY.
I DREAM OF THINGS THAT NEVER WERE
AND SAY WHY NOT.
— JOHN F. KENNEDY

*Jack Welch,* the great CEO for General Electric, "got it." Whenever and wherever he had the opportunity to sell his vision he did it. In fact, compare the various speeches he gave throughout his 21-year career and look for the common themes:

In 1983 – "Our objective, without question, is to become the most competitive enterprise on this earth. We can't be fat. We can't be bureaucratic. We can't be slow moving. We must change. We can stand for nothing less than the best. You have great responsibilities, but you also have tremendous opportunities."

In 1985 – "As we look to the next five years, our combination of different business cultures and shared values gives GE the ability – the flexibility – to win in world markets. It provides the bond that stimulates our people, the most important asset of an organization, to pursue a common goal – achieving excellence in everything we do."

In 1992 – "Our unending drive to build a boundary-less, high-spirited company is moving faster every day in the direction of what we want passionately to become – the world's most competitive company."

In 2000, as he said goodbye – "The GE of the future will be based on the cherished values that drive us today: mutual trust and the unending, insatiable, boundary-less thirst for the world's best ideas and best people. But the GE of the future will be a faster, bolder GE whose actions will make the company of today appear slow and tentative by comparison, a GE whose every employee will understand that success can only come from an inextricable link to the success of our customers."

As a leader, here's a question you must ask yourself. *Do I continually sell, and reinforce, our vision for the future?*

## IF WE WAIT FOR THE PERFECT ANSWER, THE WORLD WILL PASS US BY.
– JACK WELCH

# WHO PACKED YOUR PARACHUTE?

*As a leader,* do you honor and appreciate the power of WE? Do you stop to thank and recognize the members of your team? Do you consistently show an attitude of gratitude?

I recently read a great story about Captain Charles Plumb, a graduate from the Naval Academy, whose plane, after 74 successful combat missions over North Vietnam, was shot down. He parachuted to safety, but was captured, tortured and spent 2,103 days in a small box-like cell.

*After surviving the ordeal,* Captain Plumb received the Silver Star, Bronze Star, the Legion of Merit and two Purple Hearts, and returned to America and spoke to many groups about his experience and how it compares to the challenges of every day life.

Shortly after coming home, Charlie and his wife were sitting in a restaurant. A man rose from a nearby table, walked over and said, "You're Plumb! You flew jet fighters in Vietnam from the aircraft carrier Kitty Hawk. You were shot down!"

Surprised that he was recognized, Charlie responded, "How in the world did you know that?" The man replied, *"I packed your parachute."* Charlie looked up with surprise. The man pumped his hand, gave a thumbs-up, and said, "I guess it worked!"

Charlie stood to shake the man's hand, and assured him, "It most certainly did work. If it had not worked, I would not be here today."

Charlie could not sleep that night, thinking about the man. He wondered if he might have seen him and not even said, "Good morning, how are you?" He thought of the many hours the sailor had spent bending over a long wooden table in the bottom of the ship, carefully folding the silks and weaving the shrouds of each chute, each time holding in his hands the fate of someone he didn't know.

Plumb then began to realize that along with the physical parachute, he needed mental, emotional and spiritual parachutes. He had called on all these supports during his long and painful ordeal.

*As a leader, how many times a day, a week, a month, do we pass up the opportunity to thank those people in our organization who are "packing our parachutes"?*

# THE EIGHT T's

*Jim Cathcart* is a highly successful speaker and writer. Recently a friend of mine shared a short article he wrote called "The Eight T's." For me, the article clearly defined the eight elements necessary to motivate your people and grow your team. According to Jim, The Eight T's every leader should know are:

## TARGET

Know where you want to go and why. There must be a clear goal, dream or outcome which directs one's energies toward improvement. Until there is a clear target, our energies are dissipated and weakened through lack of focus.

## TOOLS

Get the tools necessary to do the job well. Without the right tools even the best artist, technician or performer would be less than they could be.

# TRAINING

Learn how to put the tools to their highest and best use. Teach them how to think about their task and how to master their craft. Talent without training doesn't form into skill.

# TIME

Take enough time to do it right. Sometimes training takes a while to sink in. Let them grow into the mastery they need. Provide the opportunity to test and develop new abilities while keeping risk to a minimum.

# TRUTH

Show them the ways in which they and their performance fit into the overall scheme. Those who only know "how" will almost always work for those who also know "why." The more you know, the higher you can go.

# TRACKING

Winners always know the score. Create a situation where they know at all times whether they are on track or not. Let them keep their own scorecard, too. As professional speaker and author Dr. Ken Blanchard says, "Feedback is the breakfast of champions."

# $\mathcal{T}$RUST

Give them room to grow. Trust them enough to allow them to exert initiative but not so much that you create great risk. No one advances until they do more than they have done before. And nobody does more than they have done before until someone else trusts them enough to give them the room to experiment and grow.

# $\mathcal{T}$OUCH

Celebrate their victories, help them learn from their failures, and inspire them to grow. Everything worthwhile is done within the context of a relationship. Without the support, encouragement and caring feedback, there is no will to persist.

Now think of someone on your team that you would like to inspire. What do you want to inspire them to do, specifically? Now look at the list of the Eight T's and determine which elements are missing. With this exercise your next steps should become obvious. ***Work to provide all eight and inspiration will come.***

# SHOW SINCERE
# APPRECIATION

I CAN GO TWO MONTHS
ON A GOOD COMPLIMENT.
– MARK TWAIN

*William James,* one of the founders of modern psychology, said, "The deepest principal in human nature is the craving to be appreciated." In fact, a study by Robert Half International found that lack of appreciation was in the top three reasons people leave companies, ahead of money and promotions. Author Michael LeBoeuf says this, "The greatest management principal in the world is…'The things that get rewarded and appreciated get done.'"

*What are some creative ways to recognize your people and show appreciation?*

Here are a few of my favorites:

**1. KNOW THEM AS PEOPLE**  Find out what's important to the people you work with. Ask about hobbies, favorite sports, ideal vacations, family, etc. This shows that you're interested in who they are in life rather than just what they are at work.

**2. WRITE THE WORD "RECOGNITION"** in your calendar/day planning system at some regular interval (like every Friday for the entire year). Make this word your trigger to quickly think of people who deserve praise. Then, immediately go thank them for their positive performance.

**3. NOTIFY THE FAMILY**  Send a letter or card to the person's spouse describing her/his performance and the positive impact it has on the organization.

**4. COMMEMORATE** the day a co-worker joined your group. Think how you'd feel receiving a hand-written note that said something like: "Hey Bob, in case you forgot, you came on board three years ago today. It's a date I won't forget because of your contributions in these three years. Thanks for being such an important member of the team."

**5. ESTABLISH A "WALL OF FAME"** Post all kinds of stuff: pictures of team members, copies of certificates of completion for training, thank you notes from customers, newspaper clippings about the organization's success, etc. Let your creativity flow … and be sure to solicit ideas from your teammates.

For appreciation to be effective, remember these three things:

➢ *It must be genuine, from the heart*

➢ *It should be specific*

➢ *It should be regular – not just special occasions.*

Celebrate with your people whenever and wherever you can. It's good for the soul … yours and theirs.

> ## LIFE CAN BE SEEN
> ### THROUGH YOUR EYES
> ## BUT IT IS NOT FULLY APPRECIATED
> ### UNTIL IT IS SEEN
> ### THROUGH YOUR HEART.
> — MARY XAVIER

WHATEVER YOU CAN DO,
OR BELIEVE YOU CAN DO, BEGIN IT.
FOR BOLDNESS HAS GENIUS,
POWER AND MAGIC IN IT.
—GOETHE

MAKE
YOUR GOALS
EXCITING

*To build great teams* you need to be highly motivated, and exciting goals will keep the "juices flowing." Goethe said, "Whatever you can do, or believe you can do, begin it. For boldness has genius, power and magic in it." Ah, yes…there is power and magic in big dreams! And, even if you may not fully reach your bigger goals, you'll still go way beyond what you might have been with a less exciting goal. Les Brown said, "Shoot for the moon. Even if you miss you'll land among the stars."

The following is a simple exercise offered by speaker and writer Jim Donovan to help you clarify your goals and begin to create the life you've always wanted.

➤ *Write what you don't want.* This will help you get a clearer idea about what you do want. Afterwards, you may want to throw this list away.

➤ *Write what you want.* List everything you want to do, be, experience, and have for the upcoming year and beyond.

➤ *Write each goal in the form of an affirmation.* Create goals in all the major areas of your life – spirituality, health, relationships, social, career, material items, and money. Next to each one, write why you want this and how you will feel when you have accomplished it.

➤ *Write at least one action you can take right now* to move toward each goal. What simple step can you take immediately?

➤ *Each day, read your list of goals,* concentrating on the feelings associated with having them – feelings such as freedom, value, love, security, safety, and prosperity. The more you can feel the feelings your goal will produce, the faster you can draw it to you.

After you reread your goals and are feeling the good feelings associated with having them, ask yourself, "What is the next action I can take to move toward this?" Do this daily and *watch your life change.*

*According to Dun & Bradstreet,* there are over 10 million businesses in the U.S. and they all have one thing in common – they were started by an entrepreneur; a person willing to bet on themselves to follow their dream.

# TEACH ENTREPRENEURIAL LEADERSHIP

*I have often compared starting a business to going through a maze.* You start with a dream and the courage to begin. You then journey through the maze, more commonly known in business circles as the "learning curve." You go…you hit a wall, you go left, you hit another wall, you go back, you hit another and another, until eventually a small light appears. It continues to get brighter as you move forward toward your goal. And with this light is a wonderful feeling. To look in the mirror and be able to say, "I took my dream to reality"…well, as the MasterCard commercials would say, is priceless.

I can also guarantee you'll need at least two partners on your journey through the maze. *Their names are Courage and Perseverance.* In fact, if someone were to ask me to pick one word to describe any success I've had in business, I wouldn't hesitate; the word would be perseverance. There have been many potholes, roadblocks and detours along the way. I also agree with Peter Drucker, who said, "WHENEVER YOU SEE A SUCCESSFUL BUSINESS, SOMEONE HAS MADE COURAGEOUS DECISIONS."

"You are out of your mind." "This is insane." "You should just get a real job." "Americans will never spend a dollar and a half for a cup of coffee." Howard Shultz heard all of the above in 1986 when he was trying to raise the money to launch Starbucks. He said, "In the course of a year, I talked to 242 investors and 217 said, 'no!' Many of them would listen to my one-hour presentation and never call me back. I'd phone, but most would not even take my call. It was a very humbling experience but my passion and unrelenting persistence eventually made it happen." One of Shultz's favorite quotes is:

> *"Care more than others think is wise;*
> *Risk more than others think is safe;*
> *Dream more than others think is practical;*
> *Expect more than others think is possible."*

My favorite definition of an entrepreneur is by George Gilder:

"They cast aside their assurance for a 40-hour week; they leave the safe cover of tenure and security … and charge across the perilous fields of change and opportunity. If they succeed, their profits will come not from what they take from their fellow citizens, but from the value they freely place on *the gift of their imagination.*"

# DEVELOP EFFECTIVE RECOGNITION PROGRAMS

*As a leader,* to "Aim for the Heart" you must make recognition a part of your culture. Mac Anderson, in his book, *Companies Don't Succeed…People Do,* describes recognition as a three-tiered process:

➤ *formal awards*

➤ *informal awards*

➤ *day-to-day awards*

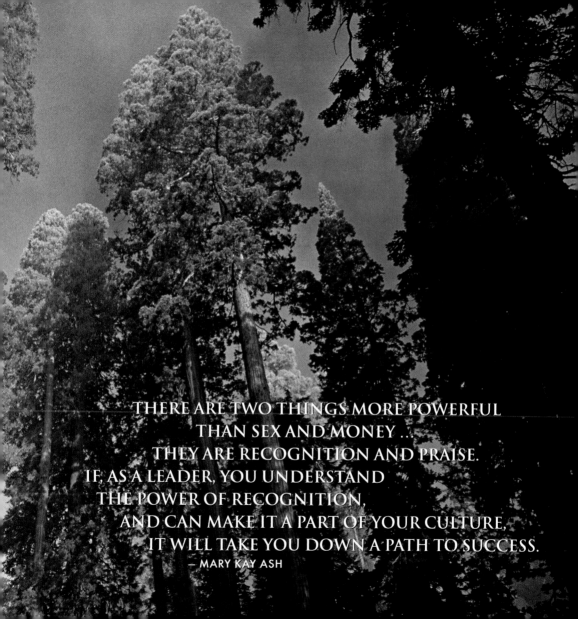

THERE ARE TWO THINGS MORE POWERFUL
THAN SEX AND MONEY ...
THEY ARE RECOGNITION AND PRAISE.
IF, AS A LEADER, YOU UNDERSTAND
THE POWER OF RECOGNITION,
AND CAN MAKE IT A PART OF YOUR CULTURE,
IT WILL TAKE YOU DOWN A PATH TO SUCCESS.
— MARY KAY ASH

> ## I DON'T DESERVE THIS AWARD,
> ## BUT I HAVE ARTHRITIS AND
> ## I DON'T DESERVE THAT EITHER.
> — JACK BENNY

# FORMAL AWARDS

These are rewards that are predetermined by management, where employees are formally recognized for their outstanding efforts. They are usually presented in front of the recipient's peers on a monthly, quarterly, or yearly basis. Examples of these awards include:

- *Employee of the Month Awards (or of the year)*
- *Salesperson of the Month Awards (or of the year)*
- *Customer Service Rep of the Month Awards (or of the year)*
- *President's Club Award (with specific criteria)*
- *Service Award (i.e. 5, 10, 15, 20, 25 years of service)*
- *Extra Mile Award*

In most cases, organizations will offer personalized awards (i.e. plaques, crystal, and other media). However, sometimes, depending on the significance of the award, other gifts of monetary value will also be given (i.e. trips, watches, a day off, cash).

# INFORMAL AWARDS

Informal award programs are designed to recognize people who have met specific goals. They are flexible, and can be tailored to meet the needs of both individuals and groups. Informal recognition can be immediate recognition given by managers to someone doing something right. They are meant to be symbolic and memorable... not costly. Examples of informal awards can be a departmental celebration, a free lunch, a gift certificate, a coffee mug, or other small gift items for the desk.

# DAY-TO-DAY AWARDS

Day-to-day awards are simple acts of kindness, gratitude and respect given from one person to another. They come in the form of written thank you notes, letters of appreciation, or positive feedback via voice mail or email. These awards or recognition play a very important role in employee satisfaction and loyalty. By far, the most effective positive feedback is both immediate and specific to the behavior being recognized.

*Never forget... recognition is a need we all crave. There are no exceptions!*

# CONQUER PROCRASTINATION

*The greatest* gap in life, according to Richard Biggs, is the one between "I should" and "I did"…more commonly known as the procrastination gap. It has been my experience that procrastination can be attitude's natural assassin. In fact, William James said, "There is nothing so fatiguing as an uncompleted task." How true it is! When you know you should do something and for whatever reason you don't, it can drift into your subconscious, drain your energy, and impact your attitude in a negative way.

As leaders we're all guilty at times, however, the key is not to develop the habit of putting things off. In fact, many potential life changing decisions are delayed endlessly because we fear failure, we're too tired, the timing isn't right, we want it to be perfect... the list goes on and on. However, I have found that the successful leaders I have met in my life are those who look for their opportunities and when they find them... *act on them*.

John Maxwell, in his book *Developing the Leader Within You*, writes about procrastination "stoppers." He calls them the three P's:

# PURPOSE

*People with a purpose in life don't procrastinate because they have something important to do. Mother Teresa, for example, had a purpose. So many people to take care of, so little time; procrastination wasn't an option.*

# PRIORITIES

*People with specific goals in life carefully rank their priorities, and are driven to accomplish their dreams.*

# PASSION

*A passion for life creates energy and a sense of urgency.*

Dr. Robert Mueller, former U.N. Assistant Secretary General, wrote the following paragraph. To me, it defines the essence of passion:

*Use every letter you write,*

*Every conversation you have,*

*Every meeting you attend*

*To express your fundamental beliefs and dreams.*

*Affirm to others the vision of the world you want.*

*You are free, an immensely powerful source of life and goodness.*

*Affirm it,*

*Spread it,*

*Radiate it!*

*Think day and night about it*

*And you will see a miracle happen,*

*The Greatness of Your Own Life.*

Find a purpose, develop your priorities, discover your passion and you will learn to bridge the greatest gap in life.

TO OPEN YOUR HEART
MEANS RISKING IT ALL –
TO EXPERIENCE GREAT JOY
AND PROFOUND SORROW.

# BE
# AUTHENTIC

*To be real, leadership must be authentic.*
Bill George, in his book *Authentic Leadership*, says it is the missing ingredient of many of today's leaders. Authentic leadership starts with integrity, values and conviction. And, a lot like the human heart, it can't be faked.

Not long ago, I read an article on the first self-contained artificial heart. What we've learned since then is fascinating. Doctors at Jewish Hospital in Louisville, Kentucky, said the recipient, a man in his 50s who had been near death until the artificial heart was implanted, could live for months or even years.

***The action of the artificial heart*** is entirely similar to the action of the natural heart. There is, however, one huge difference: the natural heart is living muscle, while the artificial heart is plastic, aluminum, and Dacron polyester. As a result, the artificial heart did not respond in the same way a human heart did.

This medical experiment was heralded as a great achievement and celebrated as a miracle. And yet, as more patients received this new technology, some of them complained that they no longer felt their emotions through their hearts. Their hearts no longer pounded deeply in their chests when they saw their loved ones. Their hearts no longer sped up when they became excited. For some patients, they would rather not survive than merely exist. Some people survive with pumps. They go through the motions of life without knowing the quickening of their own heartbeat. For some it was a life without love and without hurt, for to open your heart means risking it all – to experience great joy and profound sorrow.

Dr. Juan Asuncion said, "These programs have been bold attempts by man to duplicate the heart, given the high rate of heart disease and shortage of human hearts for transplants. While we should continue to strive to improve our quality and quantity of life, replacing the human heart with an artificial one is similar to replacing the sun with an expensive light bulb."

Opening your heart is the only way to capture the real brilliance of leadership. *Trust and respect serve as the constant unconscious heartbeats of the authentic leader.* Without these qualities, real leadership can never exist.

MAKE
**T**RUST
A MUST

TRUST MEN AND THEY
WILL BE TRUE TO YOU.
TREAT THEM GREATLY AND THEY
WILL SHOW THEMSELVES GREAT.
— RALPH WALDO EMERSON

*Building trust should be the number one priority for any leader.* Any organization without it is dead in the water. Hyler Bracey, in his book, *Be Quick or Die*, outlines a wonderful model of trust. According to Bracey, trust is a temple with four pillars: openness, honesty, credibility and respect.

OPENNESS means sharing one's thoughts and feelings and being receptive to the same in others. As openness is reciprocated, the trust level in the relationship is nudged higher.

HONESTY, as used here, means giving truthful and complete feedback – for better or worse. People want and need to know how they're doing.

CREDIBILITY means making and keeping promises.

RESPECT means honoring unspoken requests that people make in any relationship. They are:

➤ *Listen non-judgmentally*

➤ *Acknowledge differences without assigning blame*

➤ *Give credit to others for their unique and special qualities.*

When you can employ all four pillars – openness, honesty, credibility and respect – your relationships will be those of high trust.

FEW THINGS CAN HELP AN INDIVIDUAL
MORE THAN TO PLACE RESPONSIBILITY ON HIM,
AND TO LET HIM KNOW THAT YOU TRUST HIM.
– BOOKER T. WASHINGTON

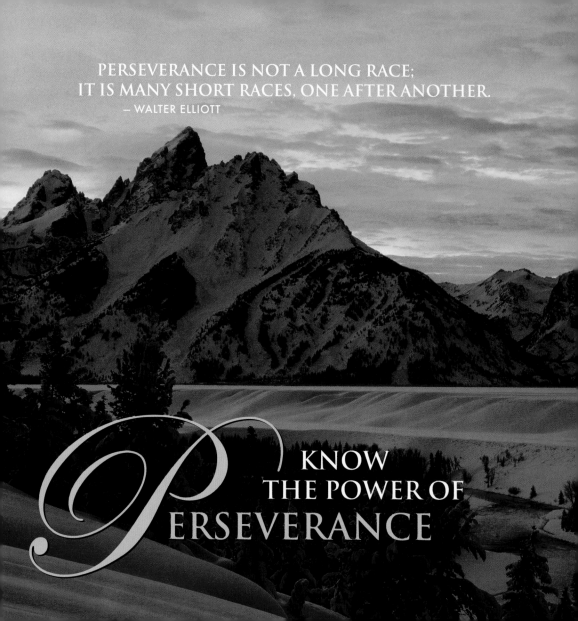

PERSEVERANCE IS NOT A LONG RACE;
IT IS MANY SHORT RACES, ONE AFTER ANOTHER.
– WALTER ELLIOTT

KNOW
THE POWER OF
PERSEVERANCE

*Carl Mays,* a speaker and author, recently shared an amazing story that I think captures the essence of leadership. I want to share it with you.

In December 1914, departing from South Georgia Island in the Atlantic Ocean, Ernest Shackleton led a crew of 27 men in a quest to cross Antarctica on foot, the last known unclaimed prize in exploration annals. As they drew within 85 miles of the continent, their ship was trapped by unusually thick ice. Originally called Polaris, the ship had been renamed Endurance by Shackleton, a term derived from his family motto, *Fortitudine Vincimus,* which means **by endurance we conquer.** This name proved to be prophetic.

Frozen fast for ten months, the trapped ship was eventually crushed and destroyed by the increasing pressure. Forced to abandon the ship, the men salvaged their lifeboats, camped on the ice for five months, and hiked to navigable waters. Amazingly, Shackleton and every crew member survived for twenty months in one of the most vicious regions of the world. They overcame extreme cold, breaking ice floes, leopard seal attacks, a shortage of food and drinking water, and, finally, two open boat trips.

The most remarkable of the small boat trips was a treacherous 800-mile ocean crossing back to South Georgia Island by Shackleton and a few of the men. Today, that achievement is considered one of the greatest navigational accomplishments in nautical history. After arriving at South Georgia, Shackleton led his team across the rugged, icy mountains, reached the island's remote whaling station, organized a rescue team, and went back for the others.

***The miraculous outcome*** against horrendous odds was attributed to Shackleton's leadership. When interviewed later, every member of the crew said they highly respected and admired Shackleton throughout the entire two-year ordeal. Shackleton never doubted they would survive and he communicated this confidence to the others. But his optimism was mixed with realism. When it became clear that the Endurance could not withstand the pressure of the ice, he made plans to abandon ship, set up camp, and search for additional possibilities. When they journeyed across the ice and Shackleton realized the need to discard weight, one of the first things to go was his valuable heirloom gold watch, which the men knew he greatly treasured. In the lifeboat journey through the frigid, stormy sea, he daringly stood in the stern of the small craft and meticulously guided its course.

**WE ARE ONE —
WE LIVE OR DIE TOGETHER.**
— ERNEST SHACKLETON

Shackleton maintained cohesion and cooperation among the men. He constantly emphasized, *"We are one – we live or die together."* He made it clear that he was in command, but he was always open to others' opinions and asked for input and suggestions. He led open discussions each evening and helped build social bonds among the men. He stressed courtesy and mutual respect. Everyone, including Shackleton, worked side by side and performed chores.

Shackleton defused anger. He wisely handled power struggles and dissidents before they could take hold, even sharing his tent with the potentially biggest dissenter. He had to alter short-term objectives and keep the men's energy on these objectives while never losing focus of the long-term goals. He found ways to lighten things up with humor and made sure there were always little successes to celebrate. His methods and actions eliminated what could have been devastating anxiety and despair among the men.

## THE DIFFERENCE BETWEEN PERSEVERANCE AND OBSTINACY IS THAT ONE COMES FROM A STRONG WILL, AND THE OTHER FROM A STRONG WON'T.
— HENRY WARD BEECHER

In the end, he knew that survival depended on a bold act, literally a do-or-die act, which was the attempt to reach an outpost by crossing 800 miles of tempestuous seas in an open boat. He took the chance. As a result, all 28 men not only survived, but they also became the epitome of the *rewards that can come from belief, creativity, and perseverance.*

# CHALLENGES

There is no thrill in easy
sailing when the skies are
clear and blue.

There is no joy in merely
doing things which
anyone can do.

But there is some satisfaction
that is mighty sweet to take.

When you reach a
destination that you thought
you couldn't make.

# REINFORCE CORE VALUES

*I was taking a plant tour* of a large company with their CEO. As we walked, I noticed many signs about the company's commitment to quality. Halfway through the tour, the CEO said, "We make it impossible for anyone not to know how we feel about quality. It's a core value that we constantly reinforce."

TRY NOT TO BECOME A MAN OF SUCCESS,
BUT RATHER A MAN OF VALUE.
— ALBERT EINSTEIN

Many leaders assume that because it is obvious that specific values benefit the company, workers will automatically understand. But the stark truth is it won't happen without relentless focus on hiring the right people and reinforcing values at every turn.

One company that understands this is the Ritz-Carlton Hotel Company, the only service company to twice capture the prestigious Malcolm Baldridge National Quality Award. Whenever possible, employees greet guests by name, they record details about guest preferences – from favorite drinks to entertainment – and use the information to custom-tailor future stays. They also attempt to solve every problem they encounter, and any Ritz-Carlton employee can spend up to $2,000 to resolve a problem on the spot.

For the 57-hotel luxury chain, it starts with hiring positive, empathetic workers who are eager to please. Next comes 20 days of training before they even set foot in the hotel.

Once they start, however, every employee carries a small card with the company's 20 core values. What happens next separates Ritz-Carlton from the "Ritz-Carlton wanna-bes." Everyday, all of the company's 25,000 employees partake in a 15 minute session to discuss (and reinforce) one of those core values. What Ritz-Carlton has learned is that leadership doesn't grow out of a prestigious title, but is earned by reinforcing values and attitudes – on a daily basis! This, in their opinion, is the only way to ensure that values are transferred into actions and behavior throughout the organization.

VALUES GROUND AN ORGANIZATION...
PROVIDING DIRECTION FOR PEOPLE
WHO FIND THEMSELVES IN
AMBIGUOUS SITUATIONS.
THEY ARE CRITICAL GUIDES
FOR MAKING DECISIONS.
– BUD BILANICH

BEGIN AT

*Home*

IF WE CONTINUALLY PRACTICE
FILLING OUR MINDS WITH THOUGHTS
OF FAITH, HOPE AND GRATITUDE,
IT WILL EVENTUALLY CROWD OUT
OUR FEARS."
— DR. NORMAN VINCENT PEALE

*In our business, building a great marketing team begins with building a great team at home.* The support of your partner in life can be one of the most important influences of your business success. The time needed to start a new business can't be underestimated. It's never easy, but it can be very exciting. However, it's so important to have the understanding, love and support from your spouse. Believe me when I say that two people working toward a common dream is far more powerful than one.

Some couples choose to work together, while others choose to support each other in their separate roles. Most commonly, the spouse who works full-time, with a steady paycheck and benefits, will afford the other time to work without the pressure.

Once a new business is up and running, some of the family benefits are:

➤ *Being able to spend more time with your children*

➤ *Increasing family income*

➤ *Providing back-up career development in case something happens to the primary income*

➤ *Improving your skill set by learning something new*

As you begin the process of building a great team, never forget that, with the unconditional love and support of your family, anything is possible. Sometimes when you're down, just hearing the words ... *"You can do it"* or *"We believe in you"* will remove the worry from your mind and replace it with faith. In fact, Dr. Norman Vincent Peale, in his book, *The Power of Positive Thinking*, says, "The first step in breaking the worry habit is simply believing you can. If we continually practice filling our minds with thoughts of faith, hope and gratitude, they will eventually crowd out our fears."

Start today. Sit with your spouse and let them know how much their support means to you. When it comes to your spouse and starting a new business, 1 + 1 truly equals 5.

# PERSONAL THANKS

Former U.S. Vice President Hubert Humphrey once said that a society is measured by how it treats those in the dawn of life, those in the shadows of life and those in the twilight of life. I sincerely believe that leaders should be measured by how they help people help themselves all along the way.

I appreciate the unconditional love and support of my family. My parents, **Tom and Jan Mathews,** gave me the home, upbringing and education to become the person I am today. My father, who passed away a few years ago, remains near to me in spirit, urging me to become a better leader and to conquer all obstacles in my path. I hope I have made him proud by following in his entrepreneurial footsteps. My mom was my first assistant and has always believed in me, even when others, including myself, may have had doubts. She is the very definition of "heartpower". I owe a huge debt to **my wife Cindy** and our **daughters Lauren and Christa** for all of the time spent away from them building our team and business and pouring my heart into this book one page at a time. Their understanding and support means the world to me and makes all of this possible. Although the time lost can never be repaid, please know that you are always close to my heart and you are the main reason I do this for my life's work. I also want to let my **siblings, Gary, Pat and Pam,** know how much they mean to me and to thank them for putting up with me all these years. You are all my best friends, my heroes and my family at the same time.

A special note of thanks to a future leader from the heart, **Michelle Johnson,** who took time out from her busy college schedule to read drafts of this book. Her thoughtful and candid insights assure me that our future is in good hands, good minds and good hearts.

My deepest appreciation to my alma mater, **St. Xavier High School** in Cincinnati, Ohio, for its steadfast commitment to excellence, not only in academics, but in every facet of its students' lives. They instilled in us a desire to be the men who dream the dreams and who lead others in making the difficult, pragmatic decisions for building up whatever part of the world in which we find ourselves working.

Most successful people will also tell you what it meant to have mentors in their life. I was fortunate enough to have many. Working with **Art and Angela Williams** in the 80s and **S. Hubert and Norma Humphrey** in the 90s was a dream come true. Art was a pioneer whose example showed us the future. Hubert was a visionary who inspired us to believe in the impossible. They took a naïve young kid right out of college and gave him the chance to learn a dream business and then to win in it. Your shining examples always showed me the way. Your hindsight became my foresight.

A great team cannot be built by one person. It takes the combined efforts of many incredible people to make this happen. My executive assistant **Angie McCart and Tim McCart** have been with us every step of the way. They are so loyal and work so hard to support us I can't imagine where we would be without them in our business and our lives.

**Pat Baird** with AegonUSA, **Tim Stonehocker, Kim Scouller, Scott Ham, Susan and Kent Davies, Bo Gibbs, Bill Pienias, Edie Craig, Nancy Moate** and **Freddie Maybury** with WFG have become friends and partners in success. They respect people, make money and have fun.

I'm grateful for **Monte Holm, Jack Linder, Xuan Nguyen, Bryce Peterson** and **Rich Thawley.** They helped start our great company along with me. We're doing something very special together.

I appreciate **Mike Anderson, Scott Batson, John Benham, Mike and Terri Burroughs, Tom Chester, Barry Clause, Pete Evans, Larry House, Gene Howerdd, Peter Huber, Mark Johnson, Jeff and Debbie Miles, Wood Montgomery** and **Andy Woodman** from the 90s. We made a great team!

**Jack Kenney, Terry Garvin, Don Cudney, Jerry Vahl, Ted Boswell, Frank DeMeno, Hayward and Karen Sawyer, Dave Parker, Jay Mather** and **Val Scarpaci** provided us with world class products and helped support the building of our team for many years. I also learned more about selling and presenting from **Ed and Tracy Atwell** in a few years than I could ever imagine. They are all the best of the best!

This all began with **Fred Johnson** coming to Cincinnati from Charlotte with a dream. **Jerry and Margaret Bortner, Dave and JoAnna Harvey, Steve and Melissa Brumbaugh** and **Chris and Geri Perrino** from our first decade were early leaders and great friends. Then **Dan Shrader, Randy Carson, Ron Leichman, Dave and Pam Colwell** and **Kip and Linda Keller** became teammates and friends. When **Bill and Peggy Mitchell** joined us I knew my wing person had arrived. We proved that with the right synergy, one plus one can equal 20,000+.

The additional alignment of senior leaders like **Greg and Lori Sorensen, Jeff and Marcy Blochowiak, Lance and Valerie Vennard, Dutch Aufderheide, Lance**

**Cansino, Marc and Carol Guerra, Mike Hughes, Nancy and Jim Hughes, Carl and Janis Kennedy, Noelle Kim, Gary Mathews, Pat McArdle, Mark and Sandie Redman, Ray Russo, Gary Saitowitz and Vanda Teixeira, Russ Watson** and **Gary Zeigler** has positioned our team to dominate in this new millennium.

And to all of those who I am so fortunate to call teammates, your dedication, strength and courage inspire me every single day. World Championship NBA Coach Phil Jackson said, *"The strength of the team is each individual member... the strength of each member is the team."* Our success is because of the people mentioned here and the thousands who are not. Words are just not enough to express my profound heartfelt appreciation to our team.

I appreciate my close friend and author **Dr. Tom Barrett** who told me I had books in me years before I began to believe and attempt this.

I am so grateful for the vision, support and encouragement of **Mac Anderson** and Simple Truths. Mac knew what this book could become and did something about what he saw. Being truly visionary is a rare trait these days. Special thanks to **Rich Nickel** who took our vision and words, and helped create the beautiful bound version you hold in your hands.

I'll never forget the contributions you all have made. These one-of-a-kind family members, teammates and friends have trusted, believed in and followed me for almost a quarter of a century.

*Win together, lose together, play together, stay together...*
*I love and appreciate you all from the bottom of my heart.*

In addition to the photos I personally took on pages 50, 60 and 110, my thanks to the great photographers whose work is featured in this book:

**Ken Jenkins** *(www.kenjenkins.com)* photos on the front cover, inside front cover, title page 4, and pages 6, 8, 10, 16, 34, 54, 82, 86, 94 and 105.

**Jim Brandenburg** *(www.jimbrandenburg.com)* photos on pages 32, 38, 46, 90 and 98.

**Steve Terrill** *(www.terrillphoto.com)* photos on pages 20, 66, 70, 74 and 78.

**Bruce Heineman** *(www.theartofnature.com)* photos on pages 102, 114 and inside back cover.

**Todd and Brad Reed** *(www.toddreedphoto.com)* photos on pages 36 and 62.

**Tom Mathews** is Senior Executive Vice Chairman and Co-Founder of World Financial Group (WFG), A Member of the AEGON Group. WFG is a financial services marketing company headquartered in Duluth, GA with offices worldwide. He has almost a quarter century of experience building teams and developing leaders in one of the largest industries in the world.

Tom's style of leading by the heart with vision has been very effective. His organization is known for their professionalism as well as their consistent growth. Tom spends his time speaking, training, inspiring and leading his team to success.

For more information, please visit *www.TomMathews.com*

# GREAT GIFT BOOKS...

## ...For Your Employees and Your Customers.

If you have enjoyed this book and wish to order additional copies; or if you would like to learn more about our full line of beautifully designed corporate gift books, please visit us at www.simpletruths.com, or, call us toll free at (800) 900-3427.

Please note that our books are **not sold in bookstores, Amazon or other retail outlets.** They can only be purchased direct from Simple Truths or a Simple Truths distributor.

We look forward to serving you.

**Call (800) 900-3427 or visit www.simpletruths.com**

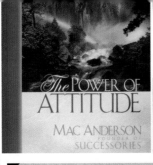
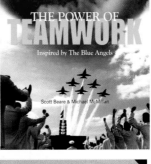
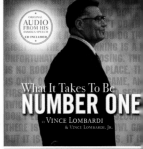

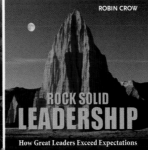

WORDS TO LIVE BY